A *Framework for* ANALYZING *the* HYDROLOGIC CONDITION *of* WATERSHEDS

by
Bruce McCammon
John Rector
Karl Gebhardt

—June 1998—

U.S. Department of Agriculture
Forest Service

U.S. Department of the Interior
Bureau of Land Management

Acknowledgments

Interagency coordination among the Forest Service (FS), Bureau of Land Management (BLM), and other agencies was essential to successful completion of this guidance. The following individuals participated on teams that developed various portions of the information contained in this document.

The core team was responsible for steering the developmental phases of this guidance and for overall coordination. The team consisted of:

Warren Harper . . . .FS
Ron Huntsinger . . . .BLM
Nancy Lopez . . . . . .U.S. Geological Survey
Larry Schmidt . . . . . .FS
Dan Muller . . . . . . .BLM
Bruce McCammon . .FS
Karl Gebhardt . . . . .BLM
John Rector . . . . . . .FS
Keith McLaughlin . . .FS
Ervin Cowley . . . . . .BLM
Doug Ryan . . . . .FS
Don Brady . . . . .Environmental Protection
                        Agency
Jack Frost . . . . .Natural Resources
                        Conservation Service

The hydrometeorological protocols team was responsible for developing national-scale basic data presentation requirements. The team was led by Keith McLaughlin and consisted of:

Dennis Murphy . . . .BLM
Dennis Kelly . . . . . .FS
Joe Frazier . . . . . . .BLM
Mike Solomon . . . . .FS
Lee Chavez . . . . . . .FS
Chester Novak . . . . .BLM
Mike Kuehn . . . . . . .FS
Jim Harte . . . . .BLM

The hydrologic condition protocols team was responsible for developing the overall analytic process. Initial team members faced an extremely difficult task of developing an analytic approach to be applied extensively throughout the United States. The following individuals initially consulted on this effort and were members of a team led by John Rector:

Richard Burns . . . . .FS
Jim Fogg . . . . .BLM
Leslie Reid . . . . .FS
Chris Knopp . . . . . . .FS
Bruce Zander . . . . . .Environmental Protection
                        Agency

The hydrologic unit protocol team, consisting of Bruce McCammon and Ervin Cowley, worked to adopt current national standards for delineating watersheds. Bob Pierce of USGS also provided significant contributions.

The core team extends its appreciation to individuals who assisted with documenting and preparing this guidance. These individuals include:

Penny Williams . . . . .FS
Margaret Trujillo . . . .BLM
Linda Hill . . . . .BLM
Janine Koselak . . . . . .BLM

Further acknowledgement is extended to Jim Greenfield (EPA) for his support and willingness to test and apply this guidance on the Chattooga River in Georgia.

Table of Contents ——————

Introduction —————————

Purpose

The Bureau of Land Management (BLM) and the Forest Service (FS) are responsible for managing natural resources on public lands. While the numerous resources on the public lands are diverse, they are also interrelated, which means that management actions pertaining to one resource will also impact others.

Water is one resource that has the potential to impact numerous other resources. For the BLM and FS, an important part of fulfilling their resource management responsibilities involves gaining an understanding of the physical processes that govern the flow (F), quality (Q), and/or timing (T) of water. Understanding these processes requires, among other things, information about precipitation, ground cover, vegetation, soils, geology, runoff, channels, floodplains, and riparian areas for each watershed.

Watersheds are characterized by meteorological, surface- and ground-water, and physical and biological factors functioning within the context of natural and human disturbance regimes. The flow, quality, or timing of water within a watershed is regulated by these factors. Watershed characteristics must be analyzed and interpreted using known scientific principles about hydrologic and hydrometeorological processes to describe hydrologic condition. The analysis and interpretation require basic hydrologic knowledge, knowledge of the area, and competency in using hydrologic tools and making judgments regarding hydrologic processes.

Hydrologic interpretations provide fundamental information about the linkages between terrestrial features or processes and associated aquatic or biological resources. They are intended to be combined with information developed by other disciplines to achieve an integrated and comprehensive analysis of the watershed. When merged and integrated with other resource information, hydrologic condition becomes part of the basis for identifying management opportunities and priorities, and for developing alternatives to maintain, enhance, or restore watershed function.

The purpose of this guidance is to provide a national framework for hydrologic analysis and related protocols as components of more comprehensive interdisciplinary watershed analysis. This guidance outlines a process for identifying the essential factors needed to describe hydrologic condition from a vast array of possible factors. The information assembled during the process enables those who conduct hydrologic analyses to participate effectively with other interdisciplinary team members in addressing ecosystem and resource management planning issues. The process helps to organize existing information about a watershed in the form of a watershed case file, which displays and interprets critical hydrologic information and supplements other resource information during decisionmaking processes.

Overview of the Analysis Process

Hydrologic condition analysis results in an understanding of the interrelationships among meteorological, surface- and ground-water, and physical and biological factors that influence the flow, quality, and/or timing of water. The magnitude, direction, and rate of change are the expression of hydrologic condition. The determination of hydrologic condition should, therefore, focus on the analysis of the factors that most directly influence changes in the specific watershed of interest. Watershed characteristics that are not subject to change by management activities (e.g., geology, landform, precipitation) are fundamental in defining physical limits within which management actions can be expected to influence water flow, quality, or timing. Analysis and documentation of these characteristics are needed to support interpretations of hydrologic condition and to defining the limits of management influence over the physical system.

Because watersheds vary tremendously across the country, analysts need the flexibility to select the watershed characteristics that are most relevant for the watershed they are considering. The analysis procedure outlined in this document is intended to provide the needed flexibility. The focus is on a process of analysis rather than on a prescribed or fixed set of factors that drive the analysis. This approach allows analysts to use existing tools (e.g., regional curves, nomographs) and to adapt the process based on available information (local watershed case files) and local or regional conditions and needs. It is expected that standard procedures will be used to analyze factors indicative of hydrologic condition [e.g., Techniques of Water Resources Investigations of the United States Geological Survey and An Approach to Water Resources Evaluation of Non-Point Silvicultural Sources (A Procedural Handbook - USDA)]. Use of existing information brings with it a wide range of reliability and confidence in the values. It is very important for analysts to document the level of confidence and the reliability of their estimates and conclusions. It is important to document data voids that have decreased the reliability of conclusions.

The analysis steps follow a logical sequence that will provide the basis for supporting professional estimates and judgements resulting in credible conclusions. The products of one step provide information for subsequent steps. The following steps presume that some prework has been accomplished, including delineating the watershed and assembling pertinent data:

Step 1. Characterize the watershed
Step 2. Rate factors
Step 3. Identify important factors
Step 4. Establish current levels
Step 5. Establish reference levels
Step 6. Identify changes and interpret results

The analytic process will provide a starting point for discussion of hydrologic issues, related resource issues, and questions to be addressed through ecosystem and resource management planning. The analysis is intended to be watershed-specific, dealing only with factors associated with the specific watershed being analyzed. It is likely that the analytic factors will differ between watersheds, especially watersheds in substantially different geographic settings. The expectation, however, is that within a common landscape unit, such as those defined by Bailey (1995) or Maxwell et al. (1995), the suite of important processes will likely be similar. This means that the knowledge gained in one analysis may be used to shape the next.

Analysis Preparation ——

Delineating Watersheds

Ecosystem analysis requires thinking about processes and characteristics at a variety of scales. Geographic areas are often used as the basis for analysis. Since watersheds are hierarchical, they provide a convenient structure for the analysis of hydrologic condition at a variety of geographic scales (Seaber et al. 1987).

The BLM and FS follow a standardized approach for delineating hydrologic units (watersheds) (USDA-NRCS 1995). Working cooperatively with the Natural Resources Conservation Service, U.S. Geological Survey, and other Federal and State parties, the BLM and FS delineate hydrologic unit/watersheds through the fifth code, and as necessary, the sixth code, at a scale of 1:24,000. Protocols are based on surface watershed divides. The boundaries are coordinated across state boundaries.

Analysis of hydrologic condition at larger geographic scales, such as the subbasin (fourth-level hydrologic unit), provides a broader view of conditions and important processes or factors. Analysis at larger geographic scales provides valuable context for subsequent analyses of smaller areas. Data used for analysis at the subbasin scale is more general than that used at smaller scales. Patterns and the distribution of characteristics or conditions are evident at larger scales.

The process outlined in this document is intended to be used to assess hydrologic condition of fifth- or sixth-level-code hydrologic units during land and resource management planning efforts. It is possible to complete an analysis of hydrologic condition at the watershed scale using information that is available anywhere in the United States (Core Hydrometeorological Data and Information Protocols, Appendix A). The process is intended to provide the broad context and to point to specific data and information needed for subsequent project investigations, design, prescriptions, and implementation. Analysts should resist the notion that project- or site-level data is required to complete an analysis at the watershed scale.

Developing Case Files for Core Hydrometeorological Data

Core hydrometeorological data needs to be assembled in order to gain a basic understanding of the hydrologic cycle for a watershed (see Appendix A). Principles and concepts of fundamental hydrologic processes and hydrometeorological facts are usually published and generic (i.e., change in water yield due to vegetation management). The information (e.g., annual precipitation) is universally available for larger basins and ecoregions containing important watersheds located within Federal forests and rangelands. The published principles, concepts, and hydrometeorological facts and/or their sources need to be identified, assessed, and incorporated into a watershed case file so that they can be managed on a watershed basis.

A permanent watershed case file should be developed and maintained for each watershed. These case files build a picture of the basic characteristics of the watershed. They should include trip reports; studies that relate to hydrology, geology, geomorphology, soils, or use activities; flood or storm reports; research reports; and other information that would be helpful to the analyst. The core hydrometeorological information should be included in this file, along with the hydrologic condition analysis when it is completed. The case file provides a vital source of information to current and future analysts and should be permanently maintained. (The Forest Service File Systems Handbook recognizes this need and provides for maintaining these permanent files).

Case files should be numbered by the hydrologic unit code and a watershed name. Each watershed case file should contain an index that describes the contents of the file and directs the hydrologist to additional information (e.g., large documents, maps, and access to electronic data files) (Figure 1). All data and analyses should be referenced by author, date, or location. Data collection standards and procedures should be explained. All data and analyses should provide a "version," sequence identifier (e.g., date). The files will evolve as each watershed analysis is performed. Developing full descriptive case files may take years or decades depending on the level of activity in a watershed and the priorities and resources that can be devoted to analysis.

The watershed case file will be used as a data source to assess hydrologic changes resulting from land management actions. The core hydrometeorological data is intended to improve the effectiveness of analysts as members of interdisciplinary teams, and help them provide credible advice and counsel to agency partners and other interested publics in a timely manner.

Office Location: _____

Watershed File Number/Name: _____

Hydrologic Unit Code: _____

WATERSHED CASE FILE INDEX					
	Data Gaps	Data Format	Data Location & File Name	Data Quality	Analysis Methods
METEOROLOGY Precipitation					
Air Temperature					
Evaporation					
Wind SURFACE WATER					
Quality					
Quantity GROUND WATER					
Springs and Wells					
Aquifers DRAINAGE BASIN CHARACTERISTICS					
Watershed Morphometry					
Wetlands/Riparian Areas					
Soils					
Geology					
Vegetation					
Human Influence OTHER WATERSHED-SPECIFIC DATA					

Figure 1. Watershed case file index.

The Hydrologic Condition Analysis Process

The following pages describe each step of the process in detail. An example illustrating how the process is applied and the product of each step is included. The Rio Hominy example is entirely hypothetical, and is intended to demonstrate the analysis process with some ideas for the analyst to consider. The Rio Hominy watershed has been delineated as a fifth-level hydrologic unit code watershed. This delineation was accomplished using the Federal interagency standards, as modified (USDA-NRCS 1995). Some of the factors are represented by numeric values, while other factors are described in more qualitative terms. The analyst is expected to select those factors, whether quantitative or qualitative, that are most useful for describing hydrologic condition.

In actual application, the availability of data, in addition to the experience of the analyst, will determine how each factor will ultimately be presented. The basic characterization of the watershed (Step 1) builds upon those data that should be available in the case file, along with the experience and common sense of those preparing the analysis. Other information for completing the remaining steps, particularly those supporting reference levels and interpretation, must be sought from whatever sources are available, such as research data, field data, model simulation, and/or professional knowledge and experience. Often, creativity may be required to identify and select a factor that will be useful throughout the process.

Regardless of the source of data, the analysis must be supported and documented as necessary to describe its applicability. The analysis process is designed for land use planning applications. The analysis information may be useful for other applications. Therefore, documentation of confidence, reliability, and assumptions is very important.

Step 1: Characterize the Watershed

The first step in the analysis process involves an organized documentation of what is known about the previously delineated watershed based on information available in the watershed case file. Meteorological, surface- and ground-water, physical and biological factors, and biophysical processes in the watershed should be documented. Documentation of past and current human use and development and disturbance regimes should be included. This step will provide a broad overview of the watershed. The characterization sets the stage for identifying the truly important and relevant factors that directly influence flow, quality, or timing of water in the watershed.

RIO HOMINY STEP 1: Characterize the Watershed

The following is an example characterization of the Rio Hominy watershed. This step is a summary of the hydrometeorological information provided in the Rio Hominy case file (Appendix B). Data sources are cited in the case file. If additional information is thought to be important and is included here, it should also be placed in the case file, which serves as the ultimate repository of information about the watershed.

METEOROLOGY

Precipitation
- Amount: Average annual precip = 7.0 inches at 3,000 feet mean sea level
- Type: Rain only, no snow
- Duration: Flashy—short-duration storms are common
- Frequency/Intensity: 2 yr.- 6 hour precip. = 2.5 inches
- Timing: 80% of annual precip. falls between April and June

Air Temperature
- Average annual temp = 76 °F
- Extremes = 30-120 °F

Evaporation—Exceeds precipitation at lower elevations; high evaporation rates observed at stock ponds.

Wind—40-50 mph winds (duststorms) between June and August.

SURFACE WATER

Quantity

Streams
- Avg. annual flow is 200 cfs (perennial streams)
- Annual peaks occur between April and June
- Bankfull discharge at the Grits gage (near mouth) is about 400 cfs
- Incised channel capacity at the Grits gage (near mouth) is approximately 6,000 cfs

Reservoirs and Impoundments
- Evaporation pond at mine (drainage control, 20 acre-feet)
- Stock ponds (about 50 at the 700-1,000 feet elevations, ave. size 2 acre-feet)

GROUND WATER

Springs and Wells—Major springs above mine supplying stream; water right = 2 cfs. One well at mine site (800 ft) and several agricultural wells in the lower watershed; numerous water rights exist for these wells.

Aquifer—Navajo sandstone aquifer averages 0 to 300 feet below surface; ground water plays a significant role in providing perennial flow to some lower streams. Recharge of ground water is derived from higher elevations and floodplains.

DRAINAGE BASIN CHARACTERISTICS

Watershed Morphometry (see USDA, Ecomap, 1996 for possible factors)
- Elevation range = 700 to 5,000 feet mean sea level
- Average watershed slope = 2%; slope range = 1-45%
- Watershed aspect is southwest
- 12 miles of perennial channels between 1,000 and 5,000 feet elevation
- 150 miles of intermittent/ephemeral channel, 80% of which is below 1,000 ft.
- Dendritic drainage pattern
- Watershed size = 100,000 acres

- 80% of watershed is lower than 1,000 feet; 20% is higher than 1,000 feet
- Upper stream reach gradients are between 0.5 and 1.5%, lower watershed reach gradients are < 0.5%
- 80% of the streams in the watershed are G channel type (Rosgen, 1995), 15% are C channel types, and the remainder are A channel types
- Stream channel erosion is common in the watershed
- Sheet erosion is the dominant surface erosion process

Wetlands/Riparian Areas—All wetlands are associated with streams in upper reaches and those associated with springs from the intersection of the channels and ground water. Generally, these areas are functioning at-risk, and could be improved with more establishment of deeper rooted shrubs and trees. They are classified in the National Wetland Inventory as:

- Upper Reaches
  Palustrine Scrub Shrub (80%)
  Palustrine Forested (5%)
  Palustrine Emergent (15%)
- Spring Areas
  Palustrine Scrub Shrub (80%)
  Palustrine Emergent (20%)

Soils
- Low precipitation at lower elevations results in poor soil moisture conditions.
- Soils primarily in upland areas are shallow and have low infiltration rates which cause higher amounts of runoff from these sites.

Geology—Marine sediments with inclusions of Navajo sandstone; Flagstaff limestone; volcanic peaks.

Vegetation
- Ground cover = 40%; lowland shrubs (rabbitbrush, creosote) represent 80% of existing ground cover; the remaining 20% are mesquite and palo verde
- Mesquite and palo verde trees are common in draws
- Vegetation is stagnant...old; not much carrying capacity for fire
- This is a thermally dominated system, which causes hydrophobic soil conditions and precludes extensive ground cover due to high evapotranspiration

Human Influence
- No urban development
- Cattle graze throughout the watershed
- High elevation mining; calcite exploration
- 2 active, exploratory copper mines
- 170 miles of dirt road accessing stock ponds
- Expansion of agricultural areas is beginning to impact ground water.
- 75 miles of pioneer roads to mines

Step 2: Rate Factors

The purpose of this step is to identify the truly influential factors for a given watershed. Factors displayed in Step 1 are carried into this step to be rated based on their relative influence on flow, quality, and/or timing. All factors in the characterization can, and probably do, affect flow, quality, and/or timing, but to varying degrees. The factors used in the characterization should be tabulated, and each factor's potential to influence flow, quality, and timing should be documented by rating its relative importance for the particular watershed using the scale in Table 1.

Table 1. Relative importance scale.

Rating	Relative Influence on Flow, Quality, or Timing
1	High
2	Moderate
3	Slight/none

The subjective ratings are established based on professional judgment and knowledge of the physical and biological systems within the watershed. The rating will gain strength and value if the analyst consults with other disciplines during the rating.

The ratings are relative. Factors are rated in relationship to each other. For example, all meteorological factors affect flow, quality, and/or timing—some may have a large effect and some may have only a slight effect. The same is true for water quality and quantity and other groups of factors.

The relative ratings of influence are used to help condense the wide array of possible factors into a more refined list containing only the key or controlling factors. The rationale for each rating should be documented because subsequent steps will rely on the information. The documentation also provides tracks for future analysis and facilitates response to third-party inquiries.

RIO HOMINY STEP 2: Rate Factors

Table H-1 represents the characterization factors and their relative importance in influencing flow, quality, or timing for the Rio Hominy watershed. The decisions about these factors were made with the assistance of the fisheries biologist, wetland ecologist, geologist, and U.S. Geological Survey hydrologist. The factors and their ratings should be amended by the analyst to reflect locally important watershed factors that influence water flow, quality, and timing in the watershed. The rationale for the ratings follows the table.

Table H-1. Ratings of factors that characterize the watershed (from the data in Step 1). These factors can be amended as needed to include locally relevant factors influencing flow, quality, or timing or water.

Factors	Flow	Quality	Timing
METEOROLOGY			
Precipitation			
Rain			
Amount	1	1	1
Duration	1	1	1
Frequency/Intensity	1	1	1
Air Temperature			
Monthly, Daily, Hourly			
Maximum	1	1	1
Minimum	3	3	3
Evaporation	2	1	3
Wind	3	1	3
SURFACE WATER			
Quantity			
Streams			
Floods	1	1	1
Reservoirs and Impoundments			
Natural	3	3	3
Constructed (stock ponds)	2	2	2
DRAINAGE BASIN CHARACTERISTICS			
Watershed Morphometry			
Channel Geometry (cross section)	1	2	1
Topography (slope, aspect, drainage density)	3	3	2
Wetlands/Riparian Areas	2	1	2
Soils			
Depth	1	3	1
Infiltration	1	1	1
Geology (lithology)	1	1	1
Vegetation (upland)	2	3	2
Human Influence			
Domestic Stock	2	1	3
Mining	3	1	3
Roads	2	3	2
Agriculture			
Ground-Water Extraction	1	3	3
Urban/Residential	3	3	3

Rationale for the subjective ratings in Table H-1:

METEOROLOGY

Precipitation

Rain

Amount   The total quantity of rainfall is directly related to the amount of streamflow produced by the watershed. Rainfall in the area is chemically neutral—a characteristic that influences the overall pH of the streams in the area. Runoff responds to rainfall directly due to the flashy nature of the watershed. Rainfall amount does affect water quality of the surface runoff as the result of surface erosion in the area during high-intensity storms.

Duration	The duration of rainfall is important because runoff in the Rio Hominy is flashy and responds to short-duration storm events. The amount of runoff is directly related to the duration of the storms since there is limited soil storage capacity. The short-duration storms of the area typically create a rapid response in runoff and often exceed infiltration capacity of the soils. Surface erosion and channel erosion products both influence water quality of the Rio Hominy watershed.
Frequency/ Intensity	High-intensity rainfall occurs infrequently and is associated with convective storms during the hot summer months. This high-intensity rainfall often exceeds local infiltration rates and is directly related to the amount of runoff and the rapid response of the streamflow (flashy). Local surface erosion and channel erosion directly affect the water quality of the surface runoff.

Air Temperature

Maximum	The maximum air temperature of the area (120 °F) directly influences evapo-transpiration rates in the area—high levels of evaporation from standing water (stock ponds) and strong demand for water from local vegetation. Streamflow tends to be low in the area as the result of the high ET levels. The evaporative rates also affect the total dissolved solids (TDS) of the surface water in the Rio Hominy in the immediate vicinity of the stock ponds.
Minimum	Minimum temperatures are not a controlling factor for hydrologic processes in the area.

Evaporation

Evaporation directly influences the amount of surface runoff during the hot summer months. The loss of water from the Rio Hominy due to evaporation is slight, however, due to the relatively low amount of stored surface water in the watershed. The amount of evaporation is also insignificant in terms of its ability to alter flow timing. As described above (temperature/maximum), evaporation also influences the chemical and physical water quality characteristics of the area.

Wind

Wind does not play any role in production or timing of surface runoff. It is not a major factor affecting snow distribution (no snow) and is not a major factor influencing evaporation rates. High winds do create some dust, which appears as turbidity in the runoff of the area for short periods each year.

SURFACE WATER

Quantity

Streams
  Floods

Infrequent, major flood events do occur as the result of major convective cells with sufficient development and duration to impact this watershed. When they occur, the floods have a serious and direct effect on water yield, quality, and timing.

Reservoirs &
Impoundments
  Natural

There are no natural lakes in the area.

| Constructed | Stock ponds in the area have a moderate effect on the amount of water yield from the Rio Hominy. This is due to the fact that, at the watershed scale, evaporation from the ponds is insignificant. The stock ponds have slight influence on water quality (TDS) as the result of evaporation. These effects are local and do not travel downstream in significant amounts. The stock ponds have a moderate influence on the discharge of sediment from the watershed since they offer a limited storage capacity. Temporary storage of water in the stock ponds during high-runoff periods has a moderate influence on the overall timing of water yield. Stock ponds are, however, subject to periodic overtopping and failure. |

DRAINAGE BASIN CHARACTERISTICS

Watershed Morphometry

Channel Geometry	The broad channels in the lower elevations (C channels) are characterized by a net loss of surface runoff from the area (ground-water recharge). The G channel types tend to be unstable and produce sediment by bank erosion during flashy runoff periods. The G and A channels provide an efficient network to route water from the area during high-intensity precipitation periods.
Topography	The slopes and aspects of the Rio Hominy watershed, in combination with the geology and soils of the area, regulate the type and extent of channel network development. Overall, the topography of the area does not influence the amount of water produced or the quality of the water. Topography does have a moderate effect on the timing of yield as a result of the drainage density of the watershed.
Wetlands/Riparian Areas	Riparian vegetation in the Rio Hominy has a moderate influence on water yield due to evapotranspiration rates associated with the riparian species. Since evapotranspiration rates are highest during times when the highest runoff rates occur, the effect of the riparian vegetation on the timing of water yield is only moderate. Riparian vegetation is extremely important for control of sediment from upslope sources during high runoff/surface erosion periods. Riparian vegetation is also important because it provides localized bank stability along many of the G and C channels in the area.

Soils

Depth	Shallow soils in the area have little water storage capacity, thereby directly influencing the runoff potential and timing. The shallow soils of the area do not have sufficient development to influence water quality through leaching or exchange.
Infiltration	Infiltration rates of the shallow soils in the Rio Hominy are often exceeded by rainfall intensity. This results in a direct influence on runoff amount and timing as described above. The high-intensity rainfall rates in excess of the infiltration rates drive surface erosion processes that influence local water quality (sediment and turbidity).
Geology (lithology)	Ground water from large springs is a significant component of the water yield from the Rio Hominy. This ground water also has a significant effect on the chemical water quality of the area. In addition, the springs of the area create relatively stable flow conditions during base flow periods. These are very important factors for interpreting downstream water yield, quality, and timing of flows.

Vegetation (upland)   The Rio Hominy watershed is sparsely occupied by rabbitbrush, creosote, mesquite, and palo verde. These species are phreatophytic and tend to have a high consumption of water. The old age of the vegetation, the relatively sparse density, and the lack of extensive vertical structure reduce the overall influence of the vegetation on ET rates in the watershed. At best, the density of this vegetation only has a moderate effect on the amount of water yield or timing of yield. Other than surface erosion and resultant sedimentation, there are no obvious effects of the vegetation on water quality.

Human Influence

Domestic Stock   Cattle grazing in the riparian areas is having a significant effect on water quality (bacteria and nutrients). Cattle are also trampling streambanks. This creates localized erosion and sedimentation as well as a direct change in channel form. Flow is moderately affected by localized soil compaction. Timing of flows is not affected by domestic stock.

Mining   Mines in the area are having a direct and significant influence on water quality as the result of their operations. Heavy metals are being introduced into surface waters. The mining operations do not have a discernable influence on the amount of water yield or the timing of water. Water quality problems are generated during the periods of high runoff as the result of overburden and waste disposal practices.

Roads   Due to the relatively low density of roads in the area, there are only moderate influences on water yield or timing. Effects of the roads on runoff during high-intensity storms are obvious, but can only be considered as moderate relative to the amount of water produced from direct runoff from the hillslopes of the Rio Hominy. Roads are not producing major effects on sediment production. This is because the low road density, location, and low gradients of most roads.

Agriculture
    Ground-Water
    Extraction   Increasing agriculture in the lowlands of the Rio Hominy is placing an increased demand on ground water. Since the Rio Hominy is a system that loses surface water in the low elevations, the increased demand on ground water tends to increase the demand for ground-water recharge. The net result is a loss of surface water. The enhanced ground-water recharge has a significant influence on water yield and a very limited effect on timing and water quality of surface waters.

Urban/Residential   There are no urban or residential developments in the Rio Hominy watershed.

Step 3: Identify Important Factors

After rating the factors that characterize a watershed, the analyst will identify and focus on factors for further analysis. It is anticipated that the factors used to evaluate hydrologic condition will vary from watershed to watershed. The intent is to identify the primary factors that are directly influencing flow, quality, or timing of water in the watershed being analyzed.

In addition to identifying the primary factors influencing flow, quality, and/or timing, the analyst needs to decide how to best measure or describe each factor. There are many ways to express hydrologic condition factors (e.g., flow can be represented as average annual flow, instantaneous peak flow, or as a probability estimate associated with a specific return period). The analyst needs to select a measure and metric that does the best job of relating the factor to changes in flow, quality, or timing. Ideally, the selected measure of the factor would be the one that is easiest to understand and evaluate and that best describes the factor. For example, rather than trying to evaluate all water quality variables that could be affected by grazing, the analyst might choose to describe water quality using concentrations of coliform bacteria or nutrients as the measures of water quality. The analyst may decide that these are the best measures of water quality effects associated with grazing in this watershed. The metrics chosen for coliform bacteria or nutrients might then be colonies per 100 mL and mg/L, respectively.

Where specific factors are identified that have limited or no information, the analyst should select a surrogate factor for which information exists (e.g., road density as a surrogate for infiltration reduction), collect information, or use simulation models or extrapolative techniques. The decision about which approach to take will depend on the time, funding, and resources available to do the analysis. The relative sensitivity or importance of a factor, or the measure chosen to represent it, should be considered when making a decision about how much time or energy to spend preparing the data.

Credibility and reliability of the analysis will be affected by the approach selected. Confidence and reliability of the analysis should be documented.

When selecting the primary factors for the remaining steps of the analysis, it is important to consider factors that:

+ Directly link to and greatly influence flow, quality, and timing
+ Are influenced by management
+ Are obtainable (quantifiable and/or qualifiable)
+ Reflect the dominant biophysical processes
+ Have a definable reference or range of variation over time

These considerations help the analyst to focus on how a factor was first identified and how it will be used in Steps 4, 5, and 6, but they are not meant to be used to reject a factor. They help document the logic and professional judgement used in selecting the primary factors.

Any factor in the rating table (Step 2) that has a rating of 1 for flow, quality, and/or timing should be included. Other factors with ratings of 2 or 3, or any combination thereof, may be brought forward into the analysis at the analyst's discretion. Decisions to carry forward a factor rated 2 or 3 should be based on the need for that data to analyze or interpret another factor or to support findings.

RIO HOMINY STEP 3: Identify Important Factors

Table H-1 was completed based on information from the characterization to show the relative importance of the meteorological, surface-water, ground-water, and drainage basin factors to flow, quality, and/or timing of water in the watershed. Considering the relative ratings in Table 1, several factors have been identified as the most important for the watershed.

*Factors with ratings of 1 for flow, quality, **and** timing of water:*
- Rain amount, duration, and frequency/intensity
- Maximum temperature
- Floods
- Infiltration
- Geology

*Factors with ratings of 1 for flow, quality, **or** timing of water:*
- Evaporation
- Wind
- Channel geometry
- Wetlands/riparian areas
- Soil depth
- Domestic stock
- Mining
- Ground-water extraction (agriculture)

Factors with ratings other than 1 and that the analyst has determined are relevant to the analysis:
- Constructed impoundments - Capacity and number of stock ponds are needed to support analysis of evaporation and riparian vegetation. Stock ponds are subject to failure and management influence.

Of the factors selected, the following cannot be influenced by management, but will be important descriptors to supplement and support conclusions about hydrologic conditions. Quantification of the following factors will not be necessary. Without human influence there is no variation between current and reference levels (Steps 4 and 5) that allow interpretation (Step 6):

- Rain amount, duration, frequency, and intensity
- Maximum temperature
- Floods
- Geology
- Wind

Factors that management will affect include:
- Evaporation - Stock ponds and vegetation use
- Constructed impoundments - Stock ponds
- Channel geometry - Stock trampling/chiseling of streambanks
- Wetlands/riparian areas - Grazing allotments and permits
- Soil depth - Soil compaction/erosion, stock, roads
- Infiltration - Soil compaction, roads, stock use
- Domestic stock - Grazing allotments and permits
- Copper mines - Operating plans
- Ground-water extraction - Pumping for agriculture

Table H-2 displays the measures and metrics for the factors that are influenced by management.

Table H-2. Summary of important hydrologic condition factors and selected measures.

Factor	Flow	Quality	Timing
Evaporation	Not significant	TDS (mg/L)	Not significant
Constructed impoundments	Total yield (ac-ft) Peak flow (cfs)	Sediment yield (tons/yr)	Time to peak (hr)
Channel geometry	Bankfull discharge (cfs) Bankfull width/depth ratio Average depth (ft)	Not significant	Time to peak (hr)
Wetlands/riparian areas	Not significant	Sediment yield (tons/yr)	Not significant
Soil depth	Total yield (ac-ft)	Not significant	Time to peak (hr)
Infiltration	Total yield (ac-ft) Peak flow (cfs) Minimum flow (cfs)	Sediment yield (tons/yr)	Time to peak (hr) Duration of min. flow (days)
Domestic stock	Not significant	Coliform bacteria (#/100 mL) Nutrients (mg/L)	Not significant
Mines	Not significant	Heavy metals (mg/L)	Not significant
Ground-water extraction	Total yield at mouth (ac-ft)	Not significant	Not significant

Table H-2 shows the measures of the factors to be analyzed and sources of data. Identical items in Table H-2 are grouped below.

Flow

- Total water yield (ac-ft) - The watershed is equipped with gaging stations, making this factor relatively simple to document, but its usefulness as a short-term monitoring factor is questionable. At least one gage has data prior to 1900.

- Peak flow (cfs) - The gaging station will provide good documentation for this factor.

- Bankfull discharge (cfs) - Data can be generated from several gaging station records. USGS has conducted a stream geometry study on several streams in the watershed.

- Bankfull width/depth ratio - This measure can also be used as a surrogate for flow. Other factors that may prove to be useful include bankfull width and depth, as separate factors, or perhaps flood-prone area as it relates to potential recharge during flood events.

- Average depth (ft) - This is the depth of water typically found in the channel under average annual flow conditions. It is expected to be a valuable measure for fishery considerations.

- Minimum flow (cfs) - Gaging records are available from 1900 on one gage. Old photos, journals, and newspapers provide descriptions of the channel going dry.

Quality

Water quality data from 1969 to present is available from agency monitoring programs and university studies (except heavy metals as noted below). There is little water quality data available prior to 1969. However, several streams in the region have good records and have been studied by the university, which enables development of reference data. Therefore, five factors will be useful in developing the analysis:

- TDS (mg/L)
- Sediment yield (tons/year)

- Coliform bacteria (#/100 mL)
- Nutrients (mg/L)
- Heavy metals - copper (mg/L) - mining company's permit monitoring records

Timing
- Time to peak (hr) - This data is available from streamgage record interpretations.

- Duration of minimum flow (days) - Data is currently available on several gaging stations and there is a historical record to 1900. Some descriptions are available from photos, journals, survey records, newspapers, and other accounts.

Step 4: Establish Current Levels

The next step in the process is to quantify the current range and status of the primary factors influencing flow, quality, or timing of water identified in Step 3. This is accomplished by documenting the current range of variability for each specific factor identified in Step 3. The current range of variability is considered to be the range of values that occurs during a normal cycle for the factor or process being analyzed. For most hydrologic variables or processes, this is approximately 10-15 years. Sources of information, assumptions, and the level of confidence or reliability of the current values should be documented.

RIO HOMINY STEP 4: Establish Current Levels

The numbers in Table H-3 represent a range based on hydrologic conditions over the last 10 years. Information was taken from historic records and available inventories.

Table H-3. Current range of variability for primary factors.

Factor	Value	Reliability*
Flow		
Total water yield	30,000-35,000 ac-ft	High
Peak flow (annual)	4,000-5,200 cfs	High
Bankfull discharge	4,000 cfs	Moderate
Bankfull width/depth ratio	16	Moderate
Average depth	0.3 ft	High
Minimum flow (7 day-10 yr)	0-5 cfs	High
Quality		
TDS	2,500-3,000 mg/L	High
Sediment yield	4-6 million tons/year	Moderate
Coliform bacteria	1,000-10,000 colonies/100 mL	High
Nutrients	10-30 mg/L	High
Heavy metals	1-5 mg/L	High
Timing		
Time to peak	4 hours	High
Duration of minimum flow	35-50 days	High

* Reliability is rated "high" when the values are taken from published records and/or measured data. "Moderate" ratings are used for calculated or modeled values. "Low" ratings are used when values are extrapolated, are based on broad regional relationships, or are based on assumptions or approximations.

All flow values (with the exception of bankfull discharge and width/depth ratio) are taken from published gaging records for the Grits gage at the mouth. Bankfull discharge is calculated using regional rating tables and field measurements of channel cross sections. The width/depth ratio was determined in 1982 using field surveys at miscellaneous random sites.

All quality values are based on measured values obtained by standard lab analyses (standard methods). Data sources include agency monitoring programs, university surveys, and the mining company's permit monitoring.

Timing values are derived from published USGS gaging records for the Grits gage.

Step 5: Establish Reference Levels

In order to be able to determine the rate, direction, or magnitude of change, a reference level must be established. References serve as the benchmark from which change is determined and provide a basis for comparison. A reference level is needed to explain changes in the selected factors over time as the result of human influence and natural disturbances.

Reference levels are used for comparative purposes only. They do not imply that conditions can or should move to the reference level. Reference levels are not necessarily "desired" conditions—they are simply the conditions that would be expected if the system were operating without significant human influence.

Sources of information, assumptions, and the level of confidence or reliability of the reference values should be documented. Possible sources of information about reference levels include (but are not limited to): models or simulations, extrapolation, historic records or journals, and records or studies of other areas or least disturbed areas (e.g., wilderness areas, National Parks).

RIO HOMINY STEP 5: Establish Reference Levels

The same quantifiable factors as those in step 4 are documented to allow comparison and interpretation of the change that has occurred. Examples of reference values are shown in Table H-4.

Table H-4. Reference value quantification for each selected factor.

Factor	Value	Reliability*
Flow		
Total water yield	25,000-30,000 ac-ft	Moderate
Peak flow (annual)	1,700-2,500 cfs	Moderate
Bankfull discharge	2,000 cfs	Low
Bankfull width/depth ratio	8	Low
Average depth	0.9 ft	Moderate
Minimum flow (7 day-10 yr)	5-10 cfs	Moderate
Quality		
TDS	2,000-2,300 mg/L	Low
Sediment yield	2-4 million tons/year	Low
Coliform bacteria	100-500 colonies/100 mL	Low
Nutrients (nitrogen)	0.1-0.5 mg/L	Low
Heavy metals (copper)	Not detectable	Low
Timing		
Time to peak	6 hours	Moderate
Duration of minimum flow	70-90 days	Low

* Reliability is rated "high" when the values are taken from published records and/or measured data. "Moderate" ratings are used for calculated or modeled values. "Low" ratings are used when values are extrapolated, are based on broad regional relationships, or are based on assumptions or approximations.

Sources of Information and Assumptions

Reference values for many of the flow measures were developed using the longer term historical record at the Grits gaging station. Additional measures were estimated using watershed modeling techniques provided by USGS. Cross sections were located based on three photographs taken in 1987. Measurements of these cross sections confirmed a channel geometry similar to that expected from peak flow near 2,000 cfs, which is within the range of the values found for the Grits gaging station. Average depth values were generated using average flow data extrapolated to the channel using Manning's equation. Water quality reference values were taken from similar streams in the area that have been studied by EPA.

Step 6: Identify Changes and Interpret Results

Once the current range of values and the corresponding reference level of each specific factor has been documented, the significance and causes of any observed differences between the two sets of information and the potential for recovery can be evaluated.

Significance

Significance is an interpretation by the analyst based on an evaluation of the magnitude, direction, and rate of change between current and reference values (Table 2). Ratings assigned by the analyst are subjective and are based on professional judgment and knowledge of the watershed.

Table 2. Relative significance scale.

Rating	Relative Significance
1	Significant difference
2	Moderate difference
3	Slight/no difference

Recovery

The analyst can also project the potential for recovery of the hydrologic system when the cause-effect relationship for the differences between current and reference levels are understood. Statements of cause-effect relationships need to be documented prior to rating the recovery potential. Typical "causes" of change include construction of roads, development of mining, stock use, vegetation removal or conversion, fire, insect and disease outbreaks, agricultural development, and urbanization. These causes impact the following processes: infiltration, evapotranspiration, interception, and erosion/sedimentation. Typical "effects" are increased runoff, decreased water quality, changes in streamflow timing, and alteration of channel morphology.

Ratings of recovery potential are based on knowledge of physical capability of the watershed to respond when considered within the context of social, economic, and technical feasibility and the need for recovery (Table 3). Not all change is adverse or requires correction.

Table 3. Recovery potential scale.

Rating	Recovery Potential
1	High potential
2	Moderate potential
3	Slight/no potential

A description of the logic used to arrive at the subjective ratings in Table 3 is very important. This narrative should explain how the ratings were derived, as well as explain any assumptions. The narrative is the place to document the professional understanding of the physical processes that are primarily responsible for the hydrologic condition of the watershed. The logic should be documented and retained for future use.

RIO HOMINY STEP 6: Identify Changes and Interpret Results

Cause-Effect Relationships

Presence of domestic stock has doubled the width-depth ratio through trampling/chiseling and caving of streambanks, increased peak flows through compaction, and added significant nutrient and coliform loading to the system. Roads have significant local effects on peak flows due to compaction and have decreased the time to peak flow by increasing runoff efficiency. The change in channel geometry caused by domestic stock, coupled with the increased peak flows, has resulted in sediment yield increases from channel scour, increased bankfull discharge, and reduced average depths. Continued erosion and loss of soil, coupled with increased compacted surfaces, has reduced the watershed's ability to infiltrate and store water to support base flows. Hence, the duration of minimum flows in the channels has been reduced. Stock ponds serve as minimal sediment traps. Ponds have slightly reduced water yield through increased evaporation, but the primary effect of evaporation has been increased levels of TDS. Mines have directly introduced heavy metals into the streams.

Summary Table

The information about current and reference conditions, as well as the estimated significance of these values and the recovery potential, can be easily summarized in a single table. Table H-5 organizes the data and documents the analyst's interpretation of the significance of the differences between current and reference conditions. The estimated recovery potential is also recorded in the table.

Table H-5. Summary of current and reference conditions and ratings of significance and recovery.

Factor	Current	Reference	Significance (1-3)	Recovery Potential (1-3)
Total water yield	30,000-35,000 ac-ft	25,000-30,000 ac-ft	2	2
Peak flow	4,000-5,200 cfs	1,700-2,500 cfs	1	2
Bankfull discharge	4000 cfs	2000 cfs	1	3
Bankfull width/ depth ratio	16	8	1	3
Average depth	0.3 ft	0.9 ft	1	2
Minimum flow (7 day-10 yr.)	0-5 cfs	5-10 cfs	1	3
TDS	2,500-3,000 mg/L	2,000-2,300 mg/L	3	2
Sediment yield	4-6 million t/yr	2-4 million t/yr	1	3
Coliform bacteria	1,000-10,000 colonies/100mL	100-500 colonies/100 mL	1	2
Nutrients	10-30 mg/L	0.1-0.5 mg/L	1	2
Heavy metals	1-5 mg/L	ND	1	1
Time to peak	4 hours	6 hours	3	3
Duration of min. flow	35-50 days	70-90 days	1	3

Logic for Subjective Ratings

Total Water Yield

Vegetation cover is currently 40% and the range specialists believe this can be increased to 50% with appropriate changes in allotment management. An increase in vegetation will tend to lower total water yield from the area due to increased evapotranspiration. A 10% increase in vegetation will result in an insignificant reduction of total water yield from the area.

The stock ponds trap runoff when they are in good repair, exposing the trapped water to evaporation loss. Eliminating the stock ponds would provide an insignificant amount of additional water yield. Removing the stock ponds is probably unrealistic until alternative water sources are developed for livestock or season of use changes are made. Recovery, therefore, rests with the manager's capability to implement changes in livestock management.

Peak Flow

Peak flows are increased by runoff from roads and by stock ponds that intermittently fail during flooding events. The ponds effectively store water until their poor design and construction results in a breach. Poor ground cover results in rapid runoff of rain and delivery to the stream system. Successive stock pond failures could result in a large increase in peak flow. The reduction in peak flows with removal (or proper design and construction of the stock ponds) is almost certain. The impact of the vegetation change (prior to 1950 the vegetative cover was near 50%) is clear in the gaging records, as is the impact from the stock ponds that were constructed from about 1975 on. Recovery is a function of economic incentive to repair and stabilize stock ponds, or to develop off-site water sources and remove stock ponds, or to alter livestock use by changing allotment management.

Bankfull Discharge

Channel degradation has resulted in bankfull discharge being contained within the incised channel. Time will allow the floodplain to become reestablished at a lower position (compared to the reference condition). Figure H-1 contains regional curves showing reference and current relationships between the bankfull flow and the drainage area. Alternatives to reconfiguring the incised channels are to make extremely expensive structural changes that allow the stream to be narrowed and raised in position, or to restore the channel by constructing it to its reference pattern, profile, and dimensions. A site-specific analysis of the channel and its watershed will be needed in order to determine the needed treatments. Potentially, increases in

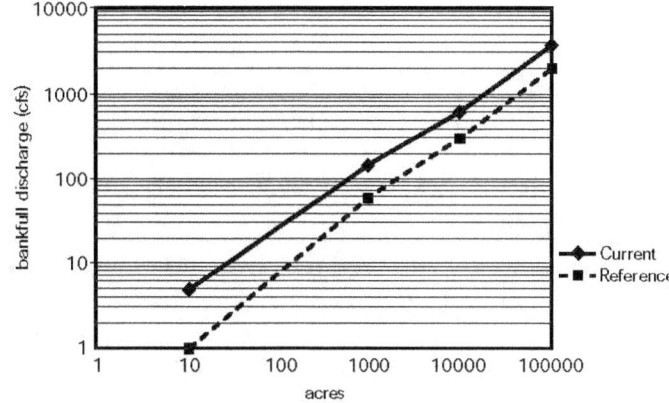

Figure H-1. Regional curves.

vegetation alone could result in aggradation significant enough to raise the floodplain to the most recent terrace. This technique has proven to be successful on other streams in the region. The prognosis for recovery in less than 10 years is poor.

Bankfull Width/Depth Ratio

The concentration of livestock along channels for water and riparian vegetation feed has contributed to severely altered channel geometry resulting in a twofold increase in the width-depth ratio. Channel geometry has also been altered by increased peak flows from road runoff, stock pond failures, soil compaction, and vegetation reduction. Excluding livestock use to eliminate chronic bank disturbance and increase vegetative cover, coupled with mechanically reconfiguring the channel, would decrease the width-depth ratio. The recovery has social implications in that the allotment has been held by the Navajo Indians for the past 50 years. Mechanical treatments, though probably limited in scope, would be very expensive.

Average Depth

The average depth is regulated by the amount of available flow and channel geometry. The existing channel has incised due to increases in peak flow and widened from livestock trampling and chiseling to the extent that normal flows are only one-third the depth of reference conditions. With modification in range use and resulting increased vegetation, stream channel geometry can be changed over time; however, the change will be slow. The average annual depth will be one of the first measures showing some short-term improvement. Establishment of vegetation, alteration of grazing practices, and limiting the failure of the stock ponds would allow streambanks to narrow and average depth to increase.

Minimum Flow

The current 7-day, 10-year low flow is less than 5 cfs. Increasing watershed cover, removing stock ponds, and improving riparian conditions would likely increase minimum flow by as much as 100%. The Grits gaging records show a relatively stable summer minimum flow until season-long grazing was implemented in 1947. Old photos, newspapers, and journal records indicate that much of the lower reaches of the Rio Hominy had perennial water, confirming the Grits gaging records. The reduction in vegetative cover and the widening of the channel has changed the ability of the watershed to store available precipitation and sustain a base flow. This has been very apparent since severe gullying has taken place, resulting in the conversion of the once active floodplains to terraces. This change has reduced the near-stream recharge from flood events, also impacting the timing and amount of low flow. The minimum flow can be changed in much the same way as the peak flow, with additional costs of channel system reconfiguration to reclaim abandoned floodplain use for recharge.

Total Dissolved Solids

The marginal increase in TDS due to stock pond evaporation and incidental inputs from mining is locally confined in the watershed. TDS could be reduced a small amount through better management of the mines; however, high evapotranspiration rates makes the stock-pond-related TDS loading difficult to manage.

Sediment Yield

Sediment yield is limiting water quality on all streams. Improving cover from 40-50%, improving maintenance procedures of stock ponds to reduce peak flows, improving mining practices, closing roads, improving road maintenance, and stabilizing the stream channels could result in significant sediment reduction. It is uncertain if these changes, if implemented, would alter the State of Arizona's report on water quality limited segments per the Clean Water Act, Section 303d. The composite remediation effort would be extremely expensive and the benefit to the listed water segments uncertain. Site-specific analysis and monitoring of the effectiveness of the practices would be required.

Coliform Bacteria

Large increases in coliform bacteria levels are attributed to season-long, unconfined grazing practices. Removing livestock or limiting livestock from the stream could significantly reduce the coliform bacteria levels. Coliform levels in ungrazed reference sites near this watershed are below 500; the coliform at these sites is attributed to wildlife and instream growth. Removing livestock has related social implications and exclusion fencing would be expensive. Adjusting the allotment to reduce the number of stock and limit the season of use would reduce coliform bacteria levels, though not as dramatically as removing stock or fencing streamside areas.

Nutrients

The agency monitoring program and university studies suggest that nutrient levels will be high in warm, low-gradient streams. Observation has confirmed that much of the lower stream segment contains algae. Removal of livestock or limiting livestock access to the streams could reduce the nutrient load. Removing livestock has related social implications and exclusion fencing would be expensive. Adjusting the allotment to reduce the number of stock and limit the season of use would reduce nutrient levels, though not as dramatically as removing stock or fencing streamside areas.

Heavy Metals

The mining company's permit records indicate copper at elevated levels in the water below the mine. Agency and university data show there are no metals in waters above the mine. Improving mining practices could eliminate this problem. Adjustments in the mine operating plan regarding overburden and waste disposal sites would reduce heavy metal loading in an economic and technically feasible manner.

Time to Peak

Change in watershed cover and changes in stock pond operation may influence the time to peak. The 2-hour increase in time to peak is not considered significant as the watershed is naturally a high-intensity storm, rapid-runoff system. Remediation to alter time to peak is unwarranted.

Duration of Minimum Flow

See the discussion under Minimum Flow.

Findings and Discussion

There are 13 factors in the Rio Hominy watershed where deviation from reference to current values is affecting hydrologic condition. Ten of the 13 factors exhibit a significant departure.

The watershed disturbance for the significant departures has been primarily tied to livestock utilization within the watershed. Reduction in vegetation resulting in accelerated erosion and increased runoff, modification of channel geometry, and constructed ponds are the primary causal agents with livestock use. Other incidental contributory disturbances include road development and mining activity.

Identified remediation opportunities include: change in grazing practices through revision of allotment management plans and permits, exclusion of stock from streambank areas with fencing and off-site water supplies, removal or reconstruction of stock ponds, mechanical configuration of channel systems, and/or elimination of livestock use within the watershed.

With the exception of reduction in heavy metals from mining, the potential to implement remediation measures is moderate to none at all. Recovery potential is constrained by high costs, social acceptability, uncertainty of end results, and questionable need for initiating recovery.

Appendix A: Core Hydrometeorological Data and Information Protocols—

The following tables present the data needed, how it should be displayed, and the procedures and/or sources that allow the display to be prepared. The tables present protocols for assessing four categories of core hydrometeorological data/information. These categories are: meteorology, surface water, ground water, and drainage basin characteristics. Other data types may be assembled, but are not considered core. Some data listed under drainage basin characteristics may be provided by other disciplines.

The basic unit for storing hydrologic data/information is the watershed case file. Data/information needs to be stored in an accessible and useable format that can be easily updated.

METEOROLOGY

DATA/INFORMATION	DISPLAY	SOURCE/PROCEDURE 1/
Precipitation (Rain and Snow) Amount	Map showing average annual precipitation.	PRIMARY SOURCE: National Oceanic and Atmospheric Administration—National Weather Service climatological data.
	Table and/or graph showing average monthly precipitation (rain and snow if applicable) for applicable climatic stations. Narrative or table for each station showing period of record, operator, frequency of sampling, Universal Transverse Mercator (UTM) coordinates, station identification number, elevation, and methods used for collection.	SUPPLEMENTAL SOURCES: State climatologist, SNOTEL, barometer watershed, research, universities, communities, schools, U.S. Forest Service and BLM files, and files from other governmental agencies (e.g., USGS, Bureau of Reclamation, NRCS).
	Table showing average maximum and minimum precipitation by month (rain and s applicable).	
Frequency and Intensity	Rainfall event intensity-frequency maps.	PRIMARY SOURCE: National Oceanic and Atmospheric Administration—National Weather Service Precipitation Frequency Atlas for applicable state.
Snow Survey	Snow pack depth and water equivalent by month for the snow season.	PRIMARY SOURCE: USDA—Natural Resources Conservation Service SNOTEL climate station summaries.

METEOROLOGY (cont.)

DATA/INFORMATION	DISPLAY	SOURCE/PROCEDURE 1/
	Narrative or table for each station showing period of record, operator, frequency of sampling, UTM coordinates, station identification number, and elevation.	SUPPLEMENTAL SOURCES: State snow survey publications.
Air Temperature	Table or graph showing monthly minimum, maximum, and average air temperature for applicable climatic stations.	PRIMARY SOURCE: National Oceanic and Atmospheric Administration—National Weather Service climatological data.
	Narrative or table for each station showing period of record, operator, frequency of sampling, UTM coordinates, station identification number, and elevation.	SUPPLEMENTAL SOURCES: State climatologist, SNOTEL, barometer watershed, research, universities, communities, schools, U.S. Forest Service and BLM files, and files from other governmental agencies (e.g., State, USGS, Bureau of Reclamation, NRCS).
Evaporation	Map of isoevaporation lines. • Annual • Seasonal	PRIMARY SOURCE: National Oceanic and Atmospheric Administration—National Weather Service Climatological Data and Evaporation Atlas.
		SUPPLEMENTAL SOURCES: State climatologist, barometer watershed, research, universities, communities, schools, U.S. Forest Service and BLM files, and files from other governmental agencies (e.g., USGS, Bureau of Reclamation).

SURFACE WATER

Quality State Water Quality Classification Designations, Standards, Beneficial Uses & Criteria, Water Quality Limited Waters	Maps, tables, and/or narratives from State water quality classification designations and standards	PRIMARY SOURCE: State Water Quality Agency or US-EPA, for the following: State water quality classifications designations and standards, 303 (d) and 305(b) reports as required by the Clean Water Act.
Surface Water Quality Data	Table showing summary of available water quality information to include: station location, period of record, water quality parameters measured.	PRIMARY SOURCE: USGS, WATSTORE database.
		SUPPLEMENTAL SOURCES: Barometer watershed, research, universities, communities, schools, U.S. Forest Service and BLM files, and files from other Federal and State agencies (e.g., USGS, Bureau of Reclamation).
Quantity Streams	Table or hydrograph showing mean monthly flow, and narrative describing low flow, high flow, extremes for period of record, station location information, and water diversions within the watershed.	PRIMARY SOURCE: USGS water resource data.
	Narrative or table for each station showing period of record, operator, frequency of sampling, UTM coordinates, station identification number, and elevation.	SUPPLEMENTAL SOURCES: Streamflow records by other Federal and State agencies and water users. Narrative interpretation of hydrograph using basin characteristics, location and quantification of water imports, exports, and diversions. Where data is not available, published regional relationships should be used.
Reservoirs and Impoundments	Map showing location and surface area.	State water rights inventories, dam engineer's inventory, and State water plan.

GROUND WATER

DATA/INFORMATION	DISPLAY	SOURCE/PROCEDURE 1/
Springs and Wells	Map of location.	PRIMARY SOURCES: Agency files for range, recreation, and administrative sites. USGS WATSTORE database. SUPPLEMENTAL SOURCES: • State water planning maps • Water users • State Engineer's office • USGS 1:24000 quads • Office of Surface Mining, etc. • Mining plans • Color infrared and other aerial photographs
Aquifers	Narrative - general description of intermediate and regional scale aquifer, noting aerial extent, depth, geologic characteristics (depth, dip, thickness, etc.) and water quality and quantity characteristics. (Option: Develop on a local basis with available data).	PRIMARY SOURCE: USGS published reports. SUPPLEMENTAL SOURCES: Office of Surface Mining, universities, State agencies, etc.

DRAINAGE BASIN CHARACTERISTICS

Watershed Morphometry	Map showing fifth- and sixth-level watershed units.	PRIMARY SOURCE: USDA—Natural Resources Conservation Service (1996) Mapping and Digitizing Watershed and Subwatershed Hydrologic Unit Boundaries. National Instruction No. 170-304 (1995, revised 1996).
Federal Classification of Water	Maps, tables, and/or narratives from Federal classifications of water, including Wild and Scenic Rivers designations, Outstanding National Resource Water designations, municipal watershed boundaries.	PRIMARY SOURCES: Maps, tables, and/or narratives for Federal classifications of water from agencies such as the Forest Service, BLM, EPA, USGS, etc.
Wetlands/Riparian Areas	Map showing wetland and riparian areas, and narrative-description of each unit.	PRIMARY SOURCE: National wetlands inventory. SUPPLEMENTAL SOURCES: Local information for soils, vegetation, and water inventories.
Soils	Maps showing soil mapping units and corresponding tables showing: • Hydrologic soil group • K factor/erosion hazard • Water-holding capacity • Growing season • Depth to ground-water table within 60 inches of surface hydric soils	PRIMARY SOURCES: NRCS soil survey reports. SUPPLEMENTAL SOURCES: Forest Service, BLM soil survey reports.
Geology	Maps and associated narratives for: • Structure • Surface rock • Lithology • Mass stability hazards • Landforms	PRIMARY SOURCES: Statewide geologic map. SUPPLEMENTAL SOURCES: USGS and State publications, soil survey reports.

DRAINAGE BASIN CHARACTERISTICS (cont.)

DATA/INFORMATION	DISPLAY	SOURCE/PROCEDURE 1/
Vegetation Cover Type	Maps and tables or narratives of the following: • Existing • Historical • Potential natural	PRIMARY SOURCES: USDA Forest Service (1977) Forest and Range Ecosystems of the U.S. Local maps and reports showing vegetation types and species. Rangeland Reform EIS. Landsat imagery, aerial photography. SUPPLEMENTAL SOURCES: Local maps, limited area project maps, and botanical studies.
Human Influence	Maps and associated narratives of roads, facilities, and urbanization. Map showing locations of climatological, streamflow, ground-water, and water qualtiy stations applicable to the watershed.	PRIMARY SOURCE: BLM and Forest Service surface management maps. PRIMARY SOURCE: See primary source under specific data type.

1/Specific sources/procedures are determined by the practitioners implementing the protocol.

Appendix B: Watershed Case File

Following is an example of the core hydrometeorological data for the Rio Hominy watershed; it would comprise the minimal amount of data for a respective watershed case file.

METEOROLOGY

Precipitation

Amounts:

Table A-1. Calcite Station: precipitation.

	Oct	Nov	Dec	Jan	Feb	Mar	Apr	May	Jun	Jul	Aug	Sep	Total
In.	0.18	0.15	0.10	0.35	0.14	0.15	1.50	2.50	1.60	0.25	0.08	0.00	7.00
%	2.57	2.14	1.43	5.00	2.00	2.14	21.43	35.71	22.86	3.57	1.14	0.00	100.00

Type: Rain only, no snow.

Station: Calcite Station, elevation 3,000 feet. Temperature and precipitation record 1956 to 1997.

Source: Climatological data for Arizona. Year, Month. National Oceanic and Atmospheric Administration, National Climatic Data Center, Asheville, NC.

Frequency and Intensity:

Table A-2. Storm frequency.

Recurrence Interval (yrs)	Storm Duration (hrs)	Precip. Amount (inches)
2	6	2.50
5	6	2.60
10	6	2.80
25	6	3.20
50	6	3.60
100	6	3.80
500	6	4.20
2	24	2.70
5	24	2.80
10	24	2.90
25	24	3.50
50	24	3.80
100	24	4.00
500	24	4.50

Source: Miller, J.F., R.H. Fredrick, and R.J. Tracy. 1973. Precipitation Frequency Atlas of the Western United States. Volume VI, Arizona. NOAA Atlas 2. U.S. Department of Commerce, National Oceanic and Atmospheric Administration, National Weather Service, Silver Spring, MD.

Air Temperature

Table A-3. Calcite Station: temperature (°F).

	Oct	Nov	Dec	Jan	Feb	Mar	Apr	May	Jun	Jul	Aug	Sep	Ave
Max	90	85	79	80	75	85	90	105	110	120	110	100	95
Min	57	50	37	35	30	45	60	70	78	82	70	69	57
Ave	74	68	58	58	53	65	75	88	94	101	90	85	76

Station and Source: See Table 1 above.

Evaporation

Display is Statewide (Arizona) evaporation map located in office library. Evaporation rates generally exceed precipitation at lower elevations. High evaporation rates have been observed at stock ponds.

Source: Jeppson, et al., 1968. Hydrologic Atlas of Arizona. Report wg 351. Arizona Water Resources Laboratory, Arizona State University, Phoenix, AZ. Evaporation Map page 53.

Wind

High winds occur June through August: 40-50 mph.

Station and Source: See Table 1 above.

SURFACE WATER

Quality

State Water Quality Classification, Standards, etc.:

The waters of the state are classed by beneficial use, and numeric standards for each class are listed. The Rio Hominy is classed for cold-water biota in the upper reach and for warm-water biota in the lower reach. Beneficial uses identified for the Rio Hominy are: cold- and warm-water fisheries (e.g., resident brown trout, speckled dace, pupfish, woundfin minnows), stock watering, mining, and wildlife (e.g., bighorn sheep, desert reptiles, turtles, coyotes). Water quality limited waters list (303d list of waters that do not attain the State water quality standards) is revised and published every 3 years. The upper reach of the Rio Hominy is limited due to existence of heavy metals, high concentrations of sediment and bacteria, and high temperatures. The lower reach of the Rio Hominy is limited due to existence of heavy metals and high concentrations of sediment and bacteria.

Source: State Water Quality Standards for Arizona.

Quantity

Streams:

Table A-4. Monthly streamflow (cfs).

Month	Oct	Nov	Dec	Jan	Feb	Mar	Apr	May	Jun	Jul	Aug	Sep
Max	120	90	60	105	75	110	2,500	8,000	3,200	375	150	83
Avg	40	30	20	25	15	19	350	1,100	425	185	120	68
Min	15	12	10	15	13	14	150	200	180	70	30	714

Station: Grits River Gage No. 09378200. Location Section 25, T. 15 N., R. 17 W., Straight Line Base and Meridian. Period of Record: 1924-1997.

Source: Water Resources Data, Arizona, Water Year 1996. U.S. Geological Survey Water Data Report AZ - 1996 - 1

Bankfull Discharge: Grits Gage = 400 cfs.

Source: BLM files.

Incised Channel Capacity: Grits gage = 6,000 cfs.

Source: BLM files.

Reservoirs and Impoundments:

Within the watershed there are 50 stock ponds ranging from 700-1,000 feet in elevation and averaging 2 acre-feet in surface area, and an evaporation pond at the mine used for drainage control with surface area equaling approximately 20 acre-feet.

Source: State water rights files.

GROUND WATER

Spring and Wells

There are major springs above the mine supplying the streams. There is one well at the mine site (at 800 feet in elevation) with water rights for 2 cfs, and agricultural wells in the lower watershed. Many water rights exist for the agricultural wells; see local watermaster for data.

Source: State water rights files.

Aquifers

The Navajo sandstone aquifer averages 0-300 feet below the surface. Ground water plays a significant role in providing perennial flow to some lower streams. Recharge of ground water is derived from higher elevations and floodplains.

Source: State of Arizona USGS surface geology map.

DRAINAGE BASIN CHARACTERISTICS

Watershed Morphometry

Accounting Code: 14120208
Area: 100,000 acres
Elevation Range: 700-5,000 feet
Watershed Aspect: southwest

Streams and Drainage:
- 12 miles of perennial channels between 1,000 and 5,000 feet in elevation
- 150 miles of intermittent/ephemeral channel; 80% of which is below 1,000 feet
- Dendritic drainage pattern - 7 miles of stream per square mile of channel
- The upper stream reach gradients are between 0.5 and 1.5%, lower stream reach gradients are <.5%
- 80% of the streams in the watershed are G channel type, 15% are C channel types, and the remainder are A channel types (channel classification procedures—Rosgen, 1995)
- Stream channel and sheet erosion common throughout watershed; channels are incised
- Average watershed slope = 2%; slope range = 1-45%

Sources:
- Forest/Ranger District: Shining National Forest/Stumpfield District
- Watersheds delineated to fifth and sixth level units are in District GIS database and hard-copy map is located in office library
- USGS topographic maps: entire watershed is covered by seven topographic maps at a scale of 1:24,000, as follows:
  - Honey Mountain
  - Bad Dog Peak
  - Desert Flat
  - Nasty Crack
  - Grits
  - Peak-a-Boo Hills
  - Bad Luck Mountain

Federal Classification of Water: None

Wetlands/Riparian Areas

All wetlands are associated with streams in upper reaches and those associated with springs from the intersection of the channels and ground water. Generally, these areas are functioning at-risk and could be improved with more establishment of deeper rooted shrubs and trees. These are classified in the National Wetland Inventory as:

    Upper Reaches
        Palustrine Scrub Shrub (80%)
        Palustrine Forested (5%)
        Palustrine Emergent (15%)
    Spring Areas
        Palustrine Scrub Shrub (80%)
        Palustrine Emergent (20%)

    Source: Forest Service/BLM inventory data.

Soils

There is a completed soil survey for the watershed. The data is digitized. Upland soils are generally shallow with moderate to low infiltration rates. Low precipitation at lower elevations results in poor soil moisture conditions. See the Forest Soil Scientist for more specific information.

    Source: USDA county soil survey report.

Geology

Marine sediments (Navajo sandstone inclusions); Flagstaff limestone; volcanic peaks.

    Source: State of Arizona USGS surface geology map.

Vegetation

Cover Types: Ground cover = 40%; lowland shrubs (rabbitbrush, creosote) represent 80% of the existing ground cover; the remaining 20% are trees (mesquite and palo verde). Mesquite and palo verde are common in draws. Vegetation is stagnant...old; not much carrying capacity for fire. This is a thermally dominated system, which causes hydrophobic soil conditions and precludes extensive ground cover due to high evapotranspiration.

Range Data: There are two range allotments with a total of 2,000 AUMS on the watershed. Navajo Indians are the permit holders. There is year-round range use. There are 50 stock ponds between 700-1,000 ft; approximately 2 ac-ft each.

    Source: District Range Conservationist's vegetation database.

Timber Inventory: There is a timber inventory completed in 1967.

    Source: District Forester's timber inventory and maps.

Human Influence

- There is no urban development
- Cattle graze throughout the watershed
- High elevation mining and calcite exploration; there are 2 active/exploratory copper mines (1,000-5,000 ft) with surface-disturbing activities covering about 15 acres
- 170 miles of native surface road accessing stock ponds
- 75 miles of pioneer roads to mines
- Expansion of agricultural areas are beginning to impact ground water

Appendix C: Interdisciplinary Team Planning—Using the Results

Hydrologic condition analysis offers a logical process for analysts to become effective members of an interdisciplinary land management planning team by providing information on:

- Current status of factors influencing flow, quality, or timing
- Reference values of the factors influencing flow, quality, or timing
- The factors relating to the potential change in flow, quality, or timing that will serve as an aid to defining potentials for water-dependent resources
- Management actions that affect water flow, quality, or timing; hence, information on management opportunities

This information, when combined with other resource information in an interdisciplinary team setting, will initiate the planning process leading to the formulation of alternatives, land allocation, and development of standards and guidelines.

Following is one more example of how analysis and interpretation might occur in an interdisciplinary setting.

Analysis

Current: A rated staff gage at bankfull flows indicates a flow of approximately 200 cfs. Estimated reliability of this flow value is high (±10%). For this watershed, bankfull flows are roughly equivalent to average annual flow (Tr = 2.3 years).

Reference: Long-term climatic characteristics of the watershed were derived from regional dendrochronology records. Based on this climatic pattern and modeled streamflow, average annual flows were historically 100 cfs. Estimated reliability of this flow value is low (±50%)

This reference value serves as a basis for comparison with current values. The comparison allows the determination of changes.

Interpretation

Management Implications: Where current values are determined to be significantly different from reference values, the cause(s) for the deviation needs to be identified. Once the cause(s) for the deviation has been identified, management opportunity(s) has been identified to alter the magnitude, direction, or rate of the deviation.

Characterization of the watershed indicated that past management activities, including fires, grazing, road construction, and mining, may have affected streamflow. Reviews of research papers and journal articles indicate that road construction is the primary activity that may have influenced flow in this watershed. Road density has increased fourfold in the watershed. It is believed that an increased runoff efficiency of surface water from road surfaces, ditches, and culverts caused an increase in the average annual flow of approximately 100 cfs. The reliability of this estimate is low (±50%).

Discussion: In an interdisciplinary team setting, the analysis results and management implications of the increased average annual flow are described for personnel with knowledge of surface-water-dependent resources to consider in regard to their resource values/needs.

The 100-cfs increase in annual flow has provided more energy to transport sediment through the system. Based on observed conditions in similar watersheds, it is believed that the increase will, over time, create straight, wide, and shallow water channels. Where increased sediment transport capacity and wide, straight, shallow channels are found by the interdisciplinary team to be desirable, a management opportunity would be to build more roads; i.e., encourage further increased average annual flow discharges. Where such channel conditions are found by the interdisciplinary team to be undesirable, the management option would be to reduce existing road density.

Potential: The potential flow, quality, or timing conditions are established by identifying the ability to alter the magnitude, direction, and rate of deviation between reference and current conditions. The extent of alteration feasible from the current condition defines the potential.

A transportation analysis available to the interdisciplinary team (health/safety/access and egress needs) indicates that 30% of the existing roads can be obliterated. Runoff modeling indicates that obliteration of 30% of the roads will reduce the average annual flow by 40 cfs; i.e., from 200 cfs to 160 cfs. Reliability of the 40 cfs is low due to model coefficients. The actual value could be ±40% different. Hence, the potential becomes an average annual flow of 160 cfs. The decision space/operational range is from the existing 200 cfs to a potential of 160 cfs.

Upon completing the six steps of hydrologic condition analysis, the analyst is prepared to interact in an interdisciplinary team discussion with the following information:

- The reference average annual flow is 100 cfs, with ±50% reliability
- The current average annual flow is 200 cfs, with ±10% reliability
- The potential average annual flow is 160 cfs, with ±50% reliability
- Roading with more sediment transport capability is causing wide, straight, and shallow channels

The stage is set to discuss the effects of the current 200 cfs average annual flow, a further increase in the average annual flow, and/or the potential 160 cfs average annual flow in regard to water-dependent resources. Discussing the pros and cons will shape viable alternative management actions to be considered throughout the planning process. The discussion includes disclosure of the reliability of the information presented.

Appendix D: Glossary—

Analyst - The person in charge of completing the hydrologic condition process. This person is expected to possess the technical competency to interpret hydrologic processes and conditions. The analyst must have sufficient knowledge of the area being analyzed and be competent in utilizing hydrologic tools and making judgments regarding hydrologic processes. The analyst is expected to utilize any information, particularly from other disciplines, that will lead to a successful analysis. The analyst is expected to develop rationale supporting professional judgment.

Analytic Factor - The meteorological; surface- or ground-water; physical, biological, biophysical; and/or human and natural disturbance regimen variable(s) that influences the flow, quality, and/or timing of water in a watershed.

Characterization - The observable, dominant processes and biophysical factors that describe the hydrologic character of a watershed. Examples include channel density, climatic setting (e.g., snow-dominated, arid), and drainage pattern. Aspects of water quality (e.g., "quick to clear after a storm," highly turbid, orange color) are also descriptive characterizations of the water resource in a watershed. Characterization could be achieved by asking, "What physiographic or aquatic features of the watershed are observable during a flight over the watershed at 10,000 feet above the highest terrain feature?"

Geomorphology - A natural physical process that is responsible for the movement and deposition of organic and inorganic materials through a watershed under the influence of gravity or water (either on the hillslope or in a channel).

Hydrologic Condition - The current state of the processes controlling the yield, timing, and quality of water in a watershed. Each physical and biologic process that regulates or influences streamflow and ground-water character has a range of variability associated with the rate or magnitude of energy and mass exchange. At any point in time, each of these processes can be defined by their current rate or magnitude relative to the range of variability associated with each process. Integration of all processes at one time represents hydrologic condition.

Hydrologic Unit - A level of a hierarchical system to describe geographic areas (Seaber, et al., 1987). Hydrologic units are used for the collection and organization of hydrologic data.

Potential - The difference between current factor values and the capability to adjust toward reference condition values is the potential. Also referred to as operating range or management decision space.

Professional Judgment - Intuitive conclusions and predictions dependent upon an analyst's training; interpretation of facts, information, and observations; and personal knowledge of the watershed being analyzed.

Reference - The range of a factor that is representative of its recent historical values prior to significant alteration of its environment. The reference could represent conditions found in a relic site or a site having had little significant disturbances, but does not necessarily represent conditions that are attainable. The purpose of references are to establish a basis for comparing what currently exists to what has existed in recent history. References can be obtained through actual data, such as paired watersheds, well-managed watersheds, or extrapolated techniques such as modeling. Sources of information include inventory and records, General Land Office and territorial surveys, settlers' and explorers' journals, ethnographic records, local knowledge, and newspapers.

Reliability - A statistical value for the quality of a measurement process.

Surrogate Factor - Proxies that are indicative of specific factors influencing water flow, quality, or timing for which there is limited or no data/information. For example, in the absence of water quality data, road density or stream crossing density may be an appropriate expression of water quality factors.

Watershed - A geomorphic area of land and water within the confines of a drainage divide. The total area above a given point on a stream that contributes flow at that point.

Watershed Function - See Hydrologic Condition.

Literature Cited————————

Bailey, R.G. 1995. Description of the Ecoregions of the United States. U.S. Department of Agriculture. Washington, DC.

Maxwell, J.R., C.J. Edwards, M.E. Jensen, S.J. Paustian, H. Parrott, D.M. Hill. 1995. A Hierarchical Framework of Aquatic Ecological Units in North America (Nearctic Zone). U.S. Department of Agriculture, Forest Service, GTR NC-176.

Rosgen, D. 1996. Applied River Morphology. Wildland Hydrology. Pagosa Springs, CO.

Seaber, P.R., F.P. Kapinos, and G.L. Knapp. 1987. Hydrologic Unit Maps, U.S. Geological Survey, WSP 2294.

U.S. Department of Agriculture, Natural Resources Conservation Service. 1995 (Revised 1996). National Instruction No. 170-304, Mapping and Digitizing Watershed and Subwatershed Hydrologic Unit Boundaries. Washington, DC.

REPORT DOCUMENTATION PAGE

Form Approved
OMB No. 0704-0188

Public reporting burden for this collection of information is estimated to average 1 hour per response, including the time for reviewing instructions, searching existing data sources, gathering and maintaining the data needed, and completing and reviewing the collection of information. Send comments regarding this burden estimate or any other aspect of this collection of information, including suggestions for reducing this burden, to Washington Headquarters Services, Directorate for Information Operations and Reports, 1215 Jefferson Davis Highway, Suite 1204, Arlington, VA 22202-4302, and to the Office of Management and Budget, Paperwork Reduction Project (0704-0188), Washington, DC 20503.

1. AGENCY USE ONLY (leave blank)	2. REPORT DATE June 1998	3. REPORT TYPE AND DATES COVERED Final

4. TITLE AND SUBTITLE

A Framework for Analyzing the Hydrologic Condition of Watersheds

5. FUNDING NUMBERS

6. AUTHOR(S)

Bruce McCammon, John Rector, and Karl Gebhardt

8. PERFORMING ORGANIZATION REPORT NUMBER

BLM/RS/ST-98/004+7210

7. PERFORMING ORGANIZATION NAME(S) AND ADDRESS(ES)

U.S. Department of the Interior
Bureau of Land Management
National Applied Resource Sciences Center
P.O. Box 25047
Denver, CO 80225-0047

10. SPONSORING/MONITORING AGENCY REPORT NUMBER

11. SUPPLEMENTARY NOTES

For document tracking purposes, this document is also known as BLM Technical Note 405.

12a. DISTRIBUTION/AVAILABILITY STATEMENT

12b. DISTRIBUTION CODE

13. ABSTRACT (Maximum 200 words)

The Bureau of Land Management and the USDA Forest Service have developed a national framework for comprehensive interdisciplinary watershed analysis. Hydrologic condition analysis requires, among other things, obtaining information about precipitation, ground cover, vegetation, soils, geology, runoff, channels, floodplains, and riparian areas for each watershed. The analysis results in an understanding of the interrelationships among meteorological, surface- and ground-water, and physical and biological factors that influence the flow, quality, and/or timing of water. This guidance outlines a process for identifying the essential factors needed to describe hydrologic condition, while still providing the flexibility to address site-specific characteristics.

14. SUBJECT TERMS

Watersheds
Hydrologic condition
Core hydrometeorological data

15. NUMBER OF PAGES

48 including covers

16. PRICE CODE

17. SECURITY CLASSIFICATION OF REPORT Unclassified	18. SECURITY CLASSIFICATION OF THIS PAGE Unclassified	19. SECURITY CLASSIFICATION OF ABSTRACT Unclassified	20. LIMITATION OF ABSTRACT UL

NSN 7540-01-280-5500

Standard Form 298 (Rev. 2-89)
Prescribed by ANSI Std. Z39-18
296-102